i SPY

WITH MY LITTLE EYE...

BEACH!

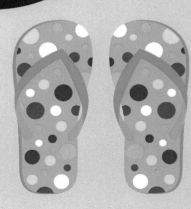

READY? LET'S BEGIN!

LET'S CONNECT:

🌐 : PamparamKidsBooks.com

▶️ : Pamparam Kids Books

📌 : Pamparam Kids Books

📷 : @PamparamKidsBooks

i SPY WITH MY LITTLE EYE, SOMETHING BEGINNING WITH...

BALL!

i SPY WITH MY LITTLE EYE, SOMETHING BEGINNING WITH...

T

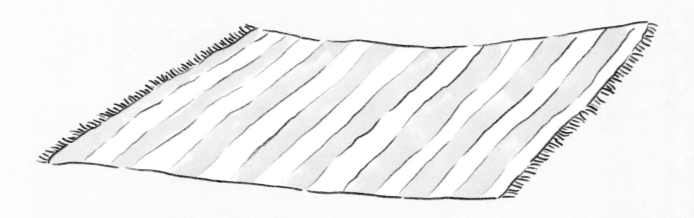

OWEL!

ICE CREAM!

I SPY WITH MY LITTLE EYE, SOMETHING BEGINNING WITH...

Coconut!

I SPY WITH MY LITTLE EYE, SOMETHING BEGINNING WITH...

FLIP-FLOPS!

i SPY WITH MY LITTLE EYE, SOMETHING BEGINNING WITH...

I SPY WITH MY LITTLE EYE, SOMETHING BEGINNING WITH...

Kite!

i SPY WITH MY LITTLE EYE, SOMETHING BEGINNING WITH...

H

Hat!

I SPY WITH MY LITTLE EYE, SOMETHING BEGINNING WITH...

I SPY WITH MY LITTLE EYE, SOMETHING BEGINNING WITH...

Fins!

i SPY WITH MY LITTLE EYE, SOMETHING BEGINNING WITH...

S

ICE CREAM

i SPY WITH MY LITTLE EYE, SOMETHING BEGINNING WITH...

U

Umbrella!

i SPY WITH MY LITTLE EYE, SOMETHING BEGINNING WITH...

I SPY WITH MY LITTLE EYE, SOMETHING BEGINNING WITH...

Girl!

i SPY WITH MY LITTLE EYE, SOMETHING BEGINNING WITH...

Watermelon!

I SPY WITH MY LITTLE EYE, SOMETHING BEGINNING WITH...

Bikini!

I SPY WITH MY LITTLE EYE, SOMETHING BEGINNING WITH...

i SPY WITH MY LITTLE EYE, SOMETHING BEGINNING WITH...

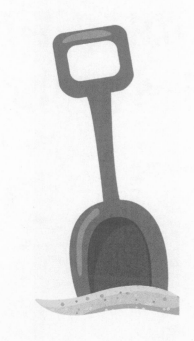

i SPY WITH MY LITTLE EYE, SOMETHING BEGINNING WITH...

GOGGLES!

Made in the USA
Monee, IL
17 March 2022

93061510R00026